CIRCUS

Deonte Osayande

Brick Mantel Books
Bloomington, Indiana

Copyright © 2018 Deonte Osayande

All rights reserved. No part of this book may be reproduced or transmitted in any form or by any means, electronic or mechanical, including photocopying, recording, or by any information storage and retrieval system, without permission in writing from the publisher.

Published by Brick Mantel Books, USA

Brick Mantel
BOOKS

www.BrickMantelBooks.com
info@BrickMantelBooks.com

An imprint of Pen & Publish, Inc.
Bloomington, Indiana
(314) 827-6567
www.PenandPublish.com

Print ISBN: 978-1-941799-55-0
eBook ISBN: 978-1-941799-56-7

Library of Congress Control Number: 2018930997

Printed on acid-free paper.

Big Top

Dinner Discussions

My aquarium breathed family enjoys
cooking crab legs. I crawl into my corner
of the house during many gatherings, eating lemons

like apples, familiar with the taste of bitterness. My teeth
sizzle every time although I don't flinch
as if my skin was thick. I know how my words can be enough

to produce gunfire. Another day, another grand jury, another
indictment. It doesn't even come up in dinner discussions
much anymore. The conversation shifts, some cousins

start fishing for compliments. I reel back my insecurities,
thankful that I'm a rabbit's foot. Not currently facing
police who would show up here because they were called, called

because they aren't here for us. Everywhere
inside the fish tank there are reflections
looking ready to consume who they mirror.

Trumpet

The savages follow the directions
on the glowing boxes

sitting on altars
throughout the house. Their angry
orange-faced deity has broadcast

his ego in front of them
for over a decade

when they watched him
search for apprentices. Now

he's hungry for herds
of scapegoats to slaughter
for his followers. They consume
whatever feeds film him, whatever
he feeds them, like blood
in the mouth of pagan vampires. They grow

violent against almost anyone
at the drop of a hat. They try to focus
on how they can trump

any person they can consider other
like me. I don't care

much about the hate or his claims
about making the country great
again. All I want is for my actions

to become brass instruments
declaring my affection
for the loved ones I would have to protect
from him and his followers.

Employment Application

For the job interview to be a success
there has to be a firm handshake

and effective work done
concealing any trace
of your ethnicity. When

getting right down to it
who you are is just too much

for the workplace to handle
when you are anything
except normal. What is this
normal that your coworkers

speak of   act like   dress like?
It's the same normal that separates

actors   athletes   musicians
from
directors   coaches   studio executives.

Everyone is ready with their
lawyers   officers   supervisors
on deck because nobody should have to deal
with the ethnic guy in the office, regardless if

he's Black   he's Asian   he's Latino
    he's Native   he's Indian
        he's of Middle Eastern descent

and lord forbid
if he's not a he.

For the job interview to be a success
you must be whatever someone else wants
with just enough you to differentiate you

from the rest of the pack
who could lose everything

to the person who doesn't need the job, just
getting hired by a relative with an opening.

Newport News

Three years after losing my grandmother we travel
down south to find my cousin on her wedding weekend
in granny's old house. The groom-to-be smiled

like a sunrise on the horizon. Everything became illuminated
when we saw how he had almost no family in attendance
our differences in skin tone became more apparent. When asked

where most of his family was
he took us to visit his relatives.
I didn't expect so many graves.

Huntsville

I wanted to be the accident uniting parents
not the one taking them away, I wanted to be
more welcomed by my mother's family,
not reasons for the graves of in-laws,
who became more tombstone than handshake.

Their vehicle became more earthquake,
where I was fault line, reason for the rush,
reason their voices became hushed,
by the crumpling crush of colliding cars.

Regret is knowing a metamorphosis of metals
would have never happened if you hadn't come,
hadn't been here to meet the family you never knew,
hadn't been garnered here to grip them as the grief came,
hadn't been born and raised in two different locations.

Torn, like having to say good bye to someone before you met,
like an introduction preceded by an obituary, torn,
like being the tremor beneath belly, the butterfly in stomach,
the child that got away, the child that came back, the child they never met.

The Firebreather Speaks of Spells

Spelling used to be a strength of mine. I'm cursed
with transforming into an earthquake

when everyone around me appears
to be an antique shop. This witchcraft will forge

fault lines across my face as I grow
older and more concerned
about how I harm who I love most
with words by accident, breaking plates

instead of forming continents
out of the connections between us. When

the magic disappears I fear
how everyone will be burned at the stake

when what I say and what I mean
don't match, instead igniting
anything but what I intended.

Pegasus

I couldn't find him, the bald-headed
baritone of his voice. I looked everywhere, even
thought I caught a lead at an office way out
in the suburbs. His receptionist gave me

the specific days he worked
but when I still called I got
no answer back. Black men

don't go to therapy, don't
get to see therapists
looking like them anyway
and the fact that I had one

was a blessing I took for granted
like food and electricity. Like running
water, I didn't cherish what I had until
it was gone and here I am now trying
to trace back my steps all of these years

later. I haven't told my therapist about
him, the secret I get to keep to myself.

I get to keep knowledge of him safe, I found
Pegasus once as a child and I'm letting him
go wild for any other future black boy who needs
to see someone about their mental health
and thinks there aren't doctors for us
as if he wasn't standing right over there.

Henry Ford Hospital, 2007

Sirens help me sleep at night, giving life
during the hours where
nobody nurtures more than their fear. Not tonight,

when all the words I thought I knew
get caught in a vice grip. Even the dog
whimpered himself back into a puppy. My chest

knotted up as I inhaled bear traps. The tardy ambulance
couldn't recover all of you. It couldn't carry
the missing address book of us, what you kept hidden.

I know how your grandfather quoted a god you weren't sure
listened when you prayed, how
you brought the one who makes each morning worth it
home to meet the family. It came as no surprise

to see him at the hospital, inconsolable,
tears collecting in his beard, when
your name filled the waiting room. Your grandfather came,

found himself shocked at how much
it hurt to see your pain. We all know
how he called your love an abomination.

Circus, 2002

My depression is an elephant
in a china shop. I tell my therapist this
and he understands how I mean to say

it ruins everything. Swallowing gasoline
while learning how to smoke, this

metaphor isn't about the suicide I did or did not
plan, but rather the way I was always caught
holding my tongue. How everything I wanted to say
kept appearing so incendiary, potentially harmful

to everyone around me. I kept my mouth shut
like a trap door some hidden creature had to be
contained behind. I told him all of this, how

my life had become a circus, and he came up
with a solution. First he invited a group of us
patients to hang out together, to get to know
one another. What we saw in this crazy house

of mirrors once we saw each other didn't matter,
what mattered was for once I didn't feel

as if I was as odd anymore. My words
no longer felt threatening to everyone
around me because in comparison

they weren't all that bad. My depression returned to the cage
where it belonged, its trunk swinging, damaging
everything on its way out as I would be treated
at least until I attempted suicide out of loneliness again.

To see the Juggler turn to page 15

To see the Tightrope Walker turn to page 27

The Juggler

The Juggler Speaks of Work

She keeps her kids midair
like balls or bowling pins
between both of her jobs

and her social life. Each one
can be knocked out of her grasp
if she doesn't manage to balance
every one. They are targets
others look to take from her

but she doesn't let any of them take strikes
from outside sources. When her children,
spared of the punishment she faced
growing up, need to learn a lesson

she finds a way to teach them. When she faces
another setback in the workplace she prepares
to not be without work for long. Without a job

the kids are left starving on the street. So she juggles
all of this at once because she has no other choice.

Stolen

The night my sister got robbed, she was struck
speechless with fear. A flimsy
cabinet of dinner plates
rested in each word
of her fragile voice and you could see
the shake of them
when she spoke. Her abusive ex-boyfriend came
to protect her, for once
but I wouldn't trust him
to guard his own name. Nothing
threatened him
more than someone taking his old job.

Raven

My little brother has a whole lot of mouth. The boy
won't stop talking, squawking
as if he just hatched from an egg and is hungry

to bite off more than he can chew. My mother calls him a baby bird
hanging in a murder of crows. She's saying he flocks
to the wrong crowd of black birds

but in certain areas our lives may be dangling
from trees quite literally anyway. My mother hates
when I travel. She wants to keep me at home,

to keep the both of us safe. She knows when I'm away I walk
around the ghetto, take the bus, ride the train. Show me the hood
and I will show you a nest. I know

how to become a raven and I can recognize a vulture
when I see one. I've seen so many boys like us lose their lives
before they gain wings and learned how to fly

without anyone shedding a tear. I know how urban gravity works, why
the trap has its name. It's been hunting season
for us for hundreds of years now. Why wouldn't we know how to blend in?

Disappearing Search

My niece asks if the police ever found
my friend. I have to tell her the truth

about when black girls go missing
how they become change, small to most

of the country, forgotten. They aren't searched for
in the same way keys are. They have worth,

power, value but to most it isn't enough
to be bothered. My niece asks if it bothers me

and I have to tell her how it's been
two full calendars since

the last time we spoke, and six months ago was the last time
anyone had heard from her. When her face showed up

on the news that December morning I still couldn't believe
what I was seeing, considering how she didn't live anywhere near

here. I remember our first time meeting, on a Greyhound bus
in Memphis, heading our separate ways. Once again,

here we are going in different directions, except
now my worry has been unlocked in ways I did not previously

know. How many black girls have had their pictures posted
online by family and friends I did not know

because they too went silently into the night? My niece
asks me if this disappearance is why I hug her so tight. I don't answer.

Traffic

The other cars on the road
cut us off, forcing
the awkward silence
associated with the wait
in the cab longer than expected
which prompts the driver
to ask what kind of people
we'd be interested in
buying
if he were selling
and this wasn't just
"an odd hypothetical."

The Firebreather Speaks of Prayer

My ashtray mouth burns
every time I tell someone
how I will pray for them

because I don't ever remember
to. Their cindering cigarette lies
smoke up my tongue. They
choke me before I can ask

for blessings, before I start confessing
to how I gave up believing
there would be someone
understanding how
the unanswered prayers

ember on the inside until their glow
goes cold. Without hellfire in my mouth
my faith stays frozen, forgotten. I used to

pray every day but after so many disappointments
my knees no longer felt naturally glues to the ground,
the prayers stopped coming and instead were replaced
with what I don't know. I do wish to be a man of faith

again but every time I start to say a word I hear nothing
but cursed incantations erupting from my mouth like flames.

Cellular

If I made an app on my phone
for black love I would name it
something like did you eat
or let me know
when you made it home safely
because I need the condition
of my lover's survival
on hand, in my palm
at a moment's notice
just like how quickly
all could be lost.

Shadow Lounge, Oakland, 2015

By the time a loved one texts me
to be careful

another person has turned
body, the local police force starts

holding a press conference
combating the word

of the dead
who cannot speak

because of their actions. While I'm here
taking stages to preach reminders

to choirs about
how we aren't safe

anywhere
I have to remember

to be thankful, how that too
has become a privilege.

Onions

Lies taste like onions. Cutting the layers
when asked if I remembered
to pick up lemons at the grocery store
my plots become bloodline thick, I create them
better than screenwriting farmers. Usually I fess up

quick, not wanting to see anyone become bitter
over something so simple. I'm trying to change
but I'm this arcade of broken vending machines. I'm not good
at playing games or giving what's asked of me
when all I constantly get is to hear two cents on my bad habits
thrown in my face. Being a chessboard with missing pieces

becomes difficult because I don't know how to make the right moves
on my own. I know it takes time but I don't want to become broken,
a washing machine accepting change from others while everything
inside me mildews until the stench gets far reaching. I've gotten good

at telling my lies but I don't want to. Sometimes I forget
to say no onions on my order like an old habit, difficult to cut away
from when it's what you're used to getting, I've grown

accustomed to liars. You can always follow the smell
of their own breath, telling you the truth in what they say.

To see the Tightrope Walker turn to page 27

To see the Clowns turn to page 37

To continue adventures and see what happens next turn to page 71

The Tightrope Walker

The Tightrope Walker Speaks of Becoming a Trapeze Artist

Free-falling from the tightrope
my mother worries about my descent.

I've been my mother's boy
for too long. I'm choosing the freedom
of flipping and spinning unharnessed airborne
instead of the security of always being
in her house. She walks a thin line

as she gets older and becomes more
of an only child again, afraid
that with change she will be left alone. My mother

doesn't see how she pushes the swing
further away with each attempt at controlling
my life. Where I want to nest
becomes clearer. It isn't in her house. Where

she sees fear the opportunity for my partner
and I to catch each other midair awaits. It's a risk
she took decades ago, one she can't remember
anymore, but I have to go and love another woman
more than her. The more she clutches me the more

she claws into my skin. Each time we experience
something new we fill her with fear, despite
how we stick the landing. She thinks I'm just

throwing everything into the wind carelessly
as if I don't know the gravity
of spending the rest of my life
with the woman I love. We intend

for our lives to last a long time together
so we must know how to safely navigate
the air. My mother frightened for the fall
doesn't want me to fly on the trapeze,

as if I haven't conquered my fear of heights
years ago when I walked the rope away from her eyes
thinking of the day when I would be jumping the broom.

Negotiating Loss

I'm gaining weight in terrible,
the scale, tipped too heavy with my grief.
The fat of it doesn't negotiate.
Every time I write, another pound of loss,
a couch swallowing change,
keys to places nobody wants unlocked,
like the home with flickering lights in my chest.

Women in my sternum
have become ornaments on ships
other men captain. Something beneath my skin
still wants them to come back from the sea.
I have missing persons posters
for people I have never met
pinned up to the insides of my ribcage.

Hope is the home with flickering lights in my chest.
I wish the switches were being flipped
by an occupant other than me
but it is really the short circuiting I deal with.

Just yesterday I blamed my mother,
nobody wants a man who cares this much,
enough to make himself weak
over and over again, for something as simple as a kiss.

Shallow graveyards sit in my memory.
I never forget any times the trust has died.
It comes back up, every time I bury another one
born between me and someone else.
With every secret I tell, repeated to me by a stranger
another eulogy.

Disappointing My Mother

My mother asks her son about grandchildren, watches
like there is a cinematic cliffhanger

waiting in my answer. There aren't any sequels
on the way for box office bombs. I try

to convince my lover to stay
but if I wore makeup it'd be ruined

after becoming concerned, defeated
by how the bus arrives

at the station
before giving her a chance

to get there. Some women get tired
of holding men who become

willows, turning into trees
who were cut down prematurely. My mother

doesn't know about me, how
her son has gone missing.

Sweetness

Instead of the water
her doctor says she needs
my mother continues to drink pop
as if she could ever lose
her southern sweetness

My father has diabetes
as if she gave it to him

A clever woman, my mother
could love my father to death
if she really truly wanted to

My mother doesn't eat enough food
but somehow survives, makes sure
she has had enough sugared beverages
and when my father goes out to get her something
she only takes a little bit, lets us vultures scavenge
or leave it behind like a bunch of ungrateful kids

My mother sees conflict as a plague,
avoids it, but she talks about the rest of us
to the rest of us, her family the exhaust pipe
to her venting and it troubles us to not talk
about our problems to someone, so we gossip
and spread rumors to each other, about each other

Somehow turned into a telephone
I've become the person everyone talks to
instead of the person who waits
on the other side of their issue

My mother doesn't drink water often
although she should considering
how she has become so sweet
she's lost her honesty, says it tastes
better to kill us with kindness

Wounds

My father pursued his doctorate
and I didn't think about the way
he studied in his midtown apartment, madman
scientist. I wasn't aware of his experiments

with other women. How my mother still lived
in the only home I knew mourning a marriage

not yet deceased. Years later, I'm an adult
learning how some unions resuscitated
back from the brink carry on

like they were never on life support. The wounds
they carry did not bleed their marriage dry
but they did manifest as memories
held by the scarred children. My older siblings
knew about his affairs. If my mother brings it up

now then he conveniently doesn't remember
those transgressions against her. It is a well

she only goes to when she is furious, a survivor
recalling what almost took her life away
because she would have murdered him
if he had ever done something like that again.

Swallowing Grief

Every listening ear my father never offered
replaced by bottles of wine. The constant

pressure around me cracks my reflections
until the resemblance starts showing. When
directly in front of him his eyes see
fragile windows. This quiet man who raised me

kept his hands off as if I were made
of burning stoves. He has taught me
little about becoming a man. Our frames

where we picture me differ greatly. He proudly
puts his prodigal son on the pedestal. My father

wears blame for my failures but the size
actually fits me. It wears me down
to want him to be the one I can ask
about advice as if he hasn't already
taught me how to silently swallow my grief.

Gradual Transformations

My name becomes a disguise, makes
many transformations
out of me. To some it says immigrant, others

say ghetto, most can't pronounce it. Instead
they say crow, spade, monkey, tar baby, jungle
bunny. My first track coach pairs me against Marcel, dog

eat dog. Bark versus bite. He be beagle, I remain
rabid unless around her. She is the black girl, my girlfriend
the tortoise. I'm her hare, growing, following

her movements in every race. She doesn't lose, just
finishes significantly later than everyone else. Someone asks
if the black girl knows she has already been beaten, as if

the black girl hasn't always survived beatings. Weeks later
the two of you go skating around the corner from her home
in the suburbs. Her neighbor's dog gets loose and she runs

half a block away faster than you've ever seen. After this
burst of speed you think back to how she made the crowd
wait and watch at the track meet. Years later Marcel is in the casino

waving when he sees you. What are the odds? You can tell
he doesn't remember anything he said to you in the past. You are still
running. The black girl is still running. He is still running.

To see the Juggler turn to page 15

To see the Clowns turn to page 37

To continue to see what happens turn to page 68

The Clowns

The Clowns Speak of the Firebreather

Clowns reside in the seventh circle of hell
with faces turned white from the ashes
of who we used to be, cremated

into my yesterdays. They look
so familiar like like ex-lovers
of mine. Their stained teeth
laugh at my attempts at recovery

from all who have harmed me. When I hear
the name of one of them I can remember
how she juggled my naivety with the makeup
she used on all of her unknowing lovers. Another
received a full bouquet of roses and turned them
into a running joke, spraying her venomous words

like water. I set fire to the notebook
where I used to write my abuser
love poems and found it a week later

with strands of big curly hair covered
in the makeup she used to wear

when we we went out. I remember kissing her
on her big nose before I knew how artificial
her feelings for me were. In Michigan

Hell is just a town a few miles away
from home. In a way they are like these
memories not too far away, even though
the people have become so distant. In this
circle of brimstone my ex-lovers haunt me,

laughing and maybe that is the joke. The way
we try to escape our pasts as if it can be run from.

Gossip Girl

The first day you stop
answering her calls
search for her knives.
Remember their names,
clues; shoulder blade,
solar plexus, spine.
Somewhere on your back
is a mystery waiting to be solved,
a word unheard by your ears
and those you hold dear
are slowly distancing themselves
because of things you never said.

The Door Was Left Unlocked for Someone Else

A dead person can't answer
a phone call, so you rang
and rang waiting to hear
my voice against your eager ear.

My speakers are still playing
James Blake's "Why Don't You Call Me"
on repeat when you walk in.

The last time we looked at each other
it was as if we had never met.
You left me alone inside a house built
from circles of light, asking that I become
nothing more than a shadow of your past.

My things are here where you left me,
like an unfinished glass of orange juice,
my pulp swirls in this place
like memories left behind.

You've tried grasping my fate.
My disappearance slips
into the cracks of your wounds,
a citrus burning lingers, sweet pain.

The last thing you find
is a basket of my teeth.
These fangs are made
of dreams and nightmares you never knew of,
sinking skin deep, forcing out the goosebumps.

You lift my journal,
as if it carries a heavy
familiar weight
The first line catching your attention says
"I've learned to stop apologizing for loving those too afraid to love me
 back"
Another car rolls by stopping before the house, dropping me off.

Forbidden

I bless your heart
because you had no idea
what you were doing

loving while black. You just saw
me, a cute boy and didn't know

what you had gotten yourself into, loving
someone who spoke in slang like it was
another language you weren't fluent in. You
were a different kind of white, Maltese,
but at the end of the day, you were still

one of them. You were still white, despite
how my cock felt taboo, felt like peace
in a time where there was war and we didn't know it

yet. How this nation treats my skin
as if it were a bunker to be bombed
in the name of guarding your own
flesh. White supremacy had not yet
reared its ugly face in our lives
but it was a beast known to me, one

you had never had to experience. The first
time I got called a nigger was the first time
I understood the language it spoke and no matter

how hard I tried I couldn't help you
understand that. No matter how many

black girls you hung out with, that was the joke
you could never get, how hated we are. Even
the black girlfriends of yours knew how
they would be viewed for dating outside the race
but let me do it and it's fair play, it's congratulations

for moving beyond race for your love. You never knew
what we had to face, you probably still don't. I see you now

with your white husband. I know how you sleep, comfortable
nuzzled in his arms. I wonder if he would still love you
knowing that you had been with me? Would you understand it
then? How forbidden we are. How toxic we are to them.

The Firebreather Speaks of Stockholm Syndrome

My neck hurts from hanging on to your words
Everything you say leaves
a heavy shadow in the smokestacks
of my throat, how ashes

recall being before burning. I taste
cinders and cinnamon on your lips
until our disagreements torch
everything. I apologize
too much. I'm not sorry

enough. The damage stays with me, a singe
of regret on the tip of my tongue. You
won't let me go, even in your absence. I know
fatigue whenever I'm looking

at our old photos. I know fatigue, my voice
shows it, like a darkened cloud
billowing up a smokestack hoping someone
sees it long enough to remember to come take care
of it, even if they arrive ready to extinguish.

The Summoning

would require a microphone
for her to air out every tale

she could tell. Her voice sounds
of several whining rodents
all chiming in at the same time to spit

poems about the sad status
of their lives. With each stanza
she tries to convince herself she
isn't the pest, the problem

in her own life. She tastes of cookies
and sweets causing cavities to be excavated
from the teeth of those who kiss her

more than once. She makes you swallow
her lies, delicacies offered dozens
at a time. The kind of sunlight
her skin is attracts all kinds of miscreants
like an abandoned alleyway. She feels

small like a candle capable of burning down
so much, an electrical fire you didn't expect.

She is my ex-girlfriend, reeking of the scent
of stereotypical poet, smelling of lemon water,
incense, and first world problems. Never
talking about resolutions to struggles, the relationship

expert despite her lack of functioning connections
with people who she hasn't made love to. She looks

harmless as a box of kittens
before you forget to declaw them. She will
come back to bite you in the backside. To summon her
is to know drama and you will need a microphone,
because she loves the stage. She has to be the center

of attention, has to be where everyone directs their eyes to,
as if her whole being is one big act. Looking for the next scene
to cause, she will find some way to make everything
about her, even when there is nothing to talk about.

Offerings

A camel with a fractured spine. All of the straw
the camel was carrying. A sliver of hay

attached to a gold necklace. A gold necklace
which turns the neck of the wearer green. A trampoline

made of nerves. A book on screenwriting
for all of the scenes

you made. An anthology
of cheat codes, since everyone

should master what they're passionate
about doing. Gasoline mouthwash

and a box of matches for burning.
All of these gifts mailed to your home

address so your mother can see why
I moved on from you years ago.

Cloaking

A former professional fighter is shown on the news
dressing like a superhero without superpowers
helping people on the street. My nephew

becomes the kid within the comic book
looking up to this crime fighter. He asks me

what superpowers I would choose
if given the chance. He assumes
everyone would be able to
control their otherworldly abilities
let alone learn how to love those

parts of themselves which don't always
make life easier. He says he would pick

invisibility as sleep peels me away
from this day-to-day conversation, an instant
interruption of slumber like the others often
orbiting outside the grasp of my control. My naps

span anywhere from seconds until hours
and ten minutes later I wake up to find him
worried he bored me to sleep. How he forgets

about my powers isn't his fault. I'm my own hero
and nemesis, hidden in plain sight. A ghost

among ghosts, walking cemetery
unseen among the unseen, black

and disabled, narcolepsy does more than force sleep
on me, it gifts me with dual invisibility and curses me
with haunting dreams of death. My ex-lover didn't know

how to handle these episodes, leaving me to figure out
the way to conceal my powers on my own. I tried to

but she didn't know that with every trip she asked me to take,
every far-off drive could be my last, just one sleep episode
away from disaster. I wake up, tell my nephew I wouldn't choose

any power outside of the ones I already have. He asks me
which ones is that, and I tell him the power to dream
of a better tomorrow. To know what it's like to feel this
double cloaking, this invisibility. To know what it is
to be hated for your skin, and your powers you can't control.

To see the Juggler turn to page 15

To see the Tightrope Walker turn to page 27

To see the Animal Tamer turn to page 50

To continue onward to see what happens turn to page 65

The Animal Tamer

The Animal Tamer Speaks of Training

With enough time and pressure
elephants can turn into lions
when given the right tamers

to care for them. Once I was
slothfully lazy, taking up space

eating as if my mouth had tusks
requiring that I smack my lips
during every bite. Once I didn't

know how to speak my mind, letting
my tough skin take every insult, complaint,
and comment that others made
without making a statement

back. I heard everything and acted
like nothing ever reached my ears.

I was a coward with a small tail swinging
between my legs. Now I've been learning
how to raise my voice, and show my teeth

when the situation presents itself. Roaring
since before I felt like I just took up space

but now I feel the weight of my presence
in the lives of those I care for. I have a reason
to jump through these hoops and it is the woman

whose finger I want to put a ring of our own on,
because she is the trainer working with me to stop
being so meek. Either way I shouldn't back down,
giving up my space so easily when I am a man

who holds so much potential. I can be large
stomping over anything in my way or as loud
as I see fit. My teeth turn tusks, fangs

when I need them to because she backs up
my evolution as a person tamed by the one
they love enough to fight their weaknesses.

A lion can be tamed but first it must know
that it is a lion and this is how we fell in love.

When Trying to Create a Distraction from the Food Falling Off My Fork

I brought up how otters hold hands
when they sleep together so they won't float
away from each other during the night. That fact did its job,
the ice was now broken. I thought it was cute, she thought

I was being weird again. I brought up how most of the time
squirrels forget where they hide their nuts, she made a quick
quip about how many men do too. The awkward
silence strikes back. I try to eat and unconsciously smack

my lips when taking the first bite. I barely notice the sound
until she rolls her eyes, as if I said her dress made her look fat,
as if I wouldn't still love her larger. She asks
about my family at the convenient moment that they crossed

my mind. I tell her about my niece, her mouth a microwave, always
popping like her teeth are made out of bags
of popcorn. She smacks her lips loudly
when she eats, snores loudly when she naps, and oh god

does she talk like a tornado siren. Every morning she has to share
everything with me before school when my blankets are heaven
sent and all I want to do is bask in them. When she comes in
quiet as a mute mouse I'm sure something has taken

away her joy, and although I've found
peace the need to ask what's wrong still lingers
like an overcast shadow covering the room. When she says
she thought about how tired I am in the morning, how she never

considered that she was one of the things keeping me
up I have no choice but to give in to my compulsion to hug
her in that moment. Victories, like planets come in all shapes and sizes,
from learning how to walk to learning

when your uncle doesn't care
about the new dance your friends taught you. I tell my date
all of this and she laughs at the quirkiness of it all. When
we continue enjoying dinner I don't bring up

any more random facts, let my fear of the silence
fade. She cracks a smile in my direction, the victory,
small but significant and for once
I don't hide giving her a smile back.

Firefly

I.

The beast becomes an emerald
smear spread across the floor

as she's fleeing from the room. After
flying to fight this insect my foot falls
electric, numb from either the impact
of landing on my charger or from just

being woken up by her fear of bugs. As
she treats the open wound in my foot

shaking with pain I see
how we need each other.

II.

The bugs are even bigger than they were
in my apartment, but I kill them all. She

heals all the damage done to me by the outside
world and I defend her from all threats no matter
how big or small they may be. I may not know
everything there is to know about being a man

but I know how to defend my woman
from fireflies and all other threats

which will come our way. This insect
glowing in the middle of the night, bright
as can be might as well be another man

as I will make him a smear on the floor
in defense of my love. I may not know
how to barbecue, which fork to use
when out at a fancy dinner, or how
to properly fix a car but I can defend her
with all of the energy I have left in my body
and that has to count for something at least.

Grocery Bags

Our families keep grocery bags
underneath the sink but nobody
ever asks why we have them

but rarely use them, like the phone number
for the police or good luck charms. We don't know

if it works but better to have it and don't need it
than to need it and don't have it. We keep
grocery bags how some people keep their gods,

tucked away only for times when they are needed, prayed to
when there is a crisis, but never when things are going our
way. These prayers are able to contain so much but we only
use them to hold one thing which we could hold in our hands

like eggs filling up the grocery bag. This is how
the black girl teaches the black boy to love himself,
like a grocery bag. We find ourselves torn when
we can hold so much. We can hardly comprehend
our capacity to love. We think self-esteem and think

only of self, not complimenting those next to us, not
sharing in our secrets, not defending what is ours. We
keep our pride in ourselves tucked away, hidden
like our gods, like we fear they will be taken from us

again. They cannot take what is a part of us, this
is what we must learn from the black girls with smiles
like eternal dawn, always coming up despite the clouds
of the time. We keep grocery bags under the sink like how

we keep our real selves, stored away, hidden and sheltered,
scared that if we hold too much the bag will rip, or be taken
from our grasp. We can't lose what is a part of us, carried
along with us. Why not use it freely? It would then be serving

its purpose. It would be serving god to not keep ourselves
hidden underneath the sink, like a bag to be used on rainy days.

The Firebreather Speaks of Rescue

My damsel in distress heroically saves me
from the gravest parts of myself. She witnesses

how I destroy the city formed from my fantasies,
struggling against the infamous insecurities
within my own brain. The mad scientists within

the control room of my brain can't match her
intelligence, can't figure out how she understands,
how she knows being funnier than a comedy club
full of the best jokes I can remember helps. So

caught up in studying my issues that they don't see
how the laboratory walls are burning down, how
she has a laboratory of her own where she has
experienced the monster of becoming overwhelmed
with the wrongs within, a house fire sparked by
the beast that is my depression. Her ability to

survive transforming into that experiment
adds to her beautiful glow, which mirrors
aren't strong enough to reflect. When

struggling to bear witness to my own parallel self
on the other side of the glass it helps knowing

how there is someone who comprehends
my wicked parts. My depression is a huge
tusked beast. It blares my weakest moments
with its trunk while it burns down everything

good I have tried to do. My lover gets this, pulls
me out of the fire every time because for her

I would do the same. I would pull her out
and even when my narcolepsy gets to be
too much to handle she's there, understanding
everything I could ever need, could ever dream up.

Consumption

Dancing in the rain with my lover, finding
joy in the eye of the storm
falling apart around us. Let her tell it and I'm crazy

for loving her. Maybe I sleep like I'm in a straitjacket
but she makes more sense than a meter maid
to me. She tries to teach me
how to cook, and finds herself

shocked at how ill equipped I am
in the kitchen. Thinks, I should be able
to feed myself without going out. How

don't I know all the things out there
trying to consume me? She overlooks
how I've been stomaching my emotions

and when my thoughts are brewing
I have to deal with the heat
of the stewing tempest of tensions.

Silent Moments

We can choose a love that will courageously seek out the wounded soul.
—bell hooks

Her mouth wide open
like the segregation of stars
snores straight up
like a sputtering car engine
resting on my clothed lap.

I snore when asleep too
so it's hilarious to see her
doing it like I do. You really
love someone when you begin
to unintentionally mimic each other.

The back of her skull
resonates warmth
against my thigh
as if there is a trust
that heat can be placed there.
I kiss against her frontal lobe
where motivation rests
without waking her.
Her. Motivation.

Black Family

She made me buy a brush
before I proposed
to her. Because my hearing
troubled me I went to set
up a meeting with a doctor. The fire
didn't touch me because I had to run.

I couldn't stop with all of the running
in the house when my mother tried to brush
my hair before church. It was like a fire
was chasing me. There was a solution proposed,
that I just have it cut short from then on, set
low on my head, and even though my mama wasn't hearing

that it stayed that way. When I got older and the hearing
of my parents started to go I was still able to run
track. I remember the starting gun, on your mark, get set,
go, and I would sprint past the other runners, brushing
shoulders with them as we went. Ideas we boys proposed
on life often came like this. Life, marriage, fleeting like fire

since our lives would be just as brief. We never knew who would fire
the guns leaving us down and dead. Didn't even know if our hearing
would survive intact. I didn't even know if I would see myself propose
to a woman. My life was like a faucet whose water won't run
anymore. I thought the bill would go unpaid, another letter brushed
aside with the other junk mail. When the time came for the sunset

to come down, I realized I was just another in a set
of siblings, another relative to be given to the fire
that is our family tree. We burn all of the brush
given. During court dates, trials, and hearings
we keep our peace, preparing to run
for joy when innocent is the verdict proposed

by the law. Even when it isn't, we propose,
get married, and celebrate in being able to set
the date. We are a black family that has learned to run
off of hope. No matter if it is a candle or a wildfire,
we take that and run with it. We're not hearing
anything else. That's why buying this brush

is a big deal. I never do anything to take care of my hair
but she makes me feel like looking nice. She cares

if I have trouble listening to what people are saying.
She is the fire keeping me warm during those cold nights.

New Years in New Orleans

and we're freezing by the riverfront
waiting for the fireworks to start. We

could have been shaking from the cold or the frustration
of not finding a cab, or everything that didn't go
according to plan during our trip but it was probably
the former since it was still our first trip and spending

that time alone was worth it
all. My art gallery memory
may be partially damaged
but there are hundreds
of paintings from that

weekend of us alone. When we examined
the museum it was pointless to look
at the exhibits as if anything else mattered
except for the company we were keeping.

Warmth attracts living things
explaining the bugs we found
during the last couple of nights

when the time we shared
worked better than the fireplace.

London, May 2016

I. London, January 2006

It smelled of neglect. The body
lay next to gifts for years
before being found. Even
in death she was preparing
to give and this is what
this world does to black women.

II. London, December 2011

Her television stayed on
for about three years before
they had noticed. A movie
was made about her life story
too late for her to see it
and that is how it always goes.
The black woman as entertainment
when their lives are in danger.

III. London, December 2003

Her name was Joyce Carol Vincent
but it could have been anything
black and buried

like pearls, or oil. Let her be
any other color and there may be
songs sung at doorways for her

disappearance. Her discovery
may have been met with someone
to feel an explosion of relief

that a body was recovered. Maybe
someone would care what mouth
captured her but unfortunately

she is black, and she is woman.
The beast lives with us daily
and nobody bats an eye.

IV. London, May 2016

This was her hometown, my love, just
imagine how they would forget someone
who is just coming to visit like yourself.

To continue onward turn to page 77

Howl

She was right. Nobody would believe it
even myself. She wasn't some large Amazonian
goddess after all. We stood about the same height.
So many years spent blocking it out, doubting
if ever really happened, because this doesn't happen

to men. I remember those exact same words to me, her
voice haunting me with its phantom phrase. This
night I can't forget. How betrayed by my own cock, she
took what she wanted and left me to return to my dorm

room, confused about what just transpired. I tried
to bury it. Like a dog. Threw dirt on the memory, slept

with other women to mask the stench. After the affairs
were made public I felt betrayed but I thought we could
finally put it behind us, her disgraced, leaving the campus

made it easier. I was wrong. There was still this rotting corpse
barking in the back of my head. I ignored it, blocked it out,

told myself I was lying about my rape. Even now, I spare myself
the pain of knowledge of having my own body taken from me, used
against me because nobody would believe it could happen

to a male athlete, as if me not wanting to do it unprotected
and her forcing it on me made it alright. I tell myself I'm lying
to keep from the guilt of knowing she probably perpetuated
cycles going on in her own life, how taking could only repay

what was done to her. Doesn't change the fact she was right
about nobody believing me, even if I tried to tell it because
even I am skeptical of the details now, omitting parts
from my own memory since the pain is too strong, like a dog
who keeps coming back home even though he died long ago,

the bark doesn't rest. I keep hearing it
echo in my head, like a howl resisting
the dirt that it stays buried underneath.

How I Almost Got Killed

It was like I stood in front of a train
when my ex-girlfriend called. I almost
died, but she was closer to death than I

was and never knew it. Her face
and name came up on my phone
like a wanted poster. When I say
that death was at the nape of my neck

what I mean to say is that my fiancée
listens to Trina, Kelis, Rihanna, and
Beyonce, which is to say she listens

to the four corners of ratchet, the sainthood
of all things smash your windows out of your
car. My fiancée gunning for her, the bounty hunter

ready to claim her target in the name of her man
but wondering why she still had a place
in my phone. Honestly, I had forgotten her, blocked

out everyone who I had once loved romantically
from my mind. How they could be wishing
something terrible would happen coming between

our union was a thought that hadn't crossed my mind
but that's why she didn't also want to make a victim

out of me. My naive carelessness saved my life
because so engulfed in the joy of our union I was
clueless to these idle threats coming from our pasts. I was
used to former lovers like hobos that would just move on

and I assumed this one would also carry on with her life
without needing to become involved with mine. I was
wrong but my love wouldn't let me stay that way. She

was here to stay and ready to fight for the man
where she made a home. I called my ex, buried
our relationship and let it die because otherwise
we would both be dead at my fiancée's hands.

To continue onward to the Juggler turn to page 15

To continue onward to the Tightrope Walker turn to page 27

To continue onward to the Animal Tamer turn to page 49

Demons

I don't often dance, music is my guilty
pleasure. What I listen to is the key
to the memories I lock out, demons yet to be

exorcised. Somewhere there's a household
built with Jenga blocks. There is a marriage
held up by a support beam of twigs. There's a wife

who I haven't spoken to in years, keeping me
behind a lock and key her husband can never open. I'm the skeleton
in their basement closet and all because I didn't know

about him doesn't mean I'm innocent. I get having
demons. Somewhere there's a house
full of people I haven't talked to in years.

In a way I am still there, haunting them. It's not
what I mean to do. I try to move on from it but when I look
down at my feet, there are so many locks.

Handshakes with Firearms

Each handshake with a firearm
familiar on the day

when my mother moved my father's guns.
How they were better concealed

the times the ring came off
while he was away from home. She never knew

about the paper bag I hid that one time
in high school for someone else

as I was introduced to the instrument
of lead for the first time. She doesn't know

that I think I helped her so my father can't find them
on a day where his bottled emotions
decide to be both the game and the marksman. The truth

how I left the room after we removed them
from their old resting place, and left her

to disguise their location for times
when I sprout antlers and flannel. He used to be

paranoid that the government was secretly hunting us
as if the sirens don't give away their presence. These days
I worry that he'll leave my mother
but not for another woman.

To continue onward to the Juggler turn to page 15

To continue onward to the Clowns turn to page 37

To continue onward to the Animal Tamer turn to page 49

Gravity

I'm a planet struggling to handle the gravity of loss
when every heartbreak forms continents, carves another island
out of me. Every ocean, a memory lingering.

I don't know how to tell the voice in my head
about its body, reduced to ash and legacy. I have all the laughs
we were meant to share. I have all the advice

she was able to give me. I remember
when she lost a fight to her own coffee table
because of her own clumsy. I remember every time

she cussed me out for not taking care of myself
before everyone else. My whole world wasn't ready
for my sister to become an extinction. I trust her

with handling my prayers. Most of them recently
had been for her, because I realize I should
have given her more. The last message

from her in my phone is her checking on me
conveniently when my depression
regulated me down

to an earthquake at the bottom
of a canyon. I lost my sister and it feels like I could lose
any and everything. I'm finding it hard

to grasp how she isn't one call or text away anymore. It's one less
person I can go to when I don't know what to do. It's difficult
watching one more person become a constellation

when I'm struggling to sleep at night. They shine
so brightly losing them shifts my geography. How
should a person grieve someone

who pulled them close and held them
when they needed it? How
does a planet mourn losing its gravity?

Melt

Today I heard a music that can make the snow shine.
—David Blair

I couldn't hit a note if it were placed
right in front of me, but I continue to sing like a bird.

I can't remember if there was snow
or if the radio was on in the car that day. I don't know
if something specifically
sparked the moment we three shared, but I instantly think

of Omari singing about wanting to swallow Keisha Cole's ovaries
as the two of us cried laughing despite the cold. I've never been a fan

of the snow. It makes me sleepy. I remember telling you in a past life
I was probably a bear. For a long time you called me

your man cat. It fit because whenever I came over to
your place I curled up on my big sister's couch as if I owned everything.
    When

you went in to the hospital you gave me the keys
so I could take care of your cats. After they ate your canaries

they kept hiding from me but their purring
still sounded like the rumbling of nature's love song. I could see

the joy in their eyes when I brought you back home
months later. When David died I knew I had lost

my really cool uncle but I would not yet understand
how poets summon the rain from anywhere

except clouds. When I was first taken in I did not yet get
how writing alone could be the start of what makes us family

but now I've lost my big sister and have found
a thunderstorm I didn't know I owned. Even now, reading your poems

I see how people got captured by your raw exposed heart. The tune
of your laughter replays in my dreams like an album of hurricanes. We
    have lost

so many in such a short period of time but today I saw
a ray of sunlight melt the snow and uncover a yellow bird's

feather. I'm convinced that was you singing a note
in the royal skyline of a majestic landscape in the fantastic above.

My Little Brother Comes Back from San Antonio

My little brother is coming back
home from San Antonio
and at the airport we embrace

like a cobra's grip when it's squeezing
the life out of you, but the hug is so
tight and firm that you wouldn't know
how hours later when my dad had a stroke

our reactions differed like two countries
coming to conflict and engaging in a bloody
war. For now, all is grand. My brother meets

my fiancée who hours later
uses her nursing training
and rescues my family
from falling to pieces

while I calmly reserve all emotion, asking
what needs to be done and my brother, scared

of looking weak, goes into a corner and cries
before downing a bottle of Hennessy and partying
his woes away for the next three days. For now,

all is grand, as they exchange jokes at my expense
and I laugh but also I'm feeling that cobra again, how
my brother lies about turning up places, how he shows
on his own schedule, and gambles away his money
until there is nothing left and he has to be bailed out
by my father who will be recovering from the stroke

in no time, his walk with a cane, his mouth twisted up
like a suspension bridge when the hurricane winds
come crashing through. We are all together, prior
to the stroke, to the rehab, to the relearning how to walk

and prior to my brother having to escape to the party
life he lives, one day at a time, until it's time for me

to take him to the airport, and go to work at the same time
and I do because he is my brother after all. We are all
together for a moment before all of this and he asks

my fiancée a question, to which she laughs like a volcano
spewing out lava when he asks if I ever told her about him,
how we are complete polar opposites, but I've always got his back.

To continue onward to the Tightrope Walker turn to page 27

To continue onward to the Clowns turn to page 37

To continue onward to the Animal Tamer turn to page 49

Circus, 2016

On our first real meeting
I tell my new therapist
how I grew up in a circus

where my best friend, a bear
of a boy, bullied me
when I was younger. My real
best friend was a teddy bear

who knew all of my deepest, darkest
secrets. I tell him how my family used to be

close before our lives tore us apart
like a traveling show with a revolving door
of entertainers. My parents taught me
to swallow my words, unless I was
regurgitating an answer in a classroom

and it became toxic to the point that I believed
anything I said could be wrong, could burn down
everything. I tell my new therapist how

my depression is the elephant in the room, always
the beast crashing into everything I've built up,
tearing down the whole tent of my accomplishments,
how this same mastodon beat my father down

and a few days ago it almost convinced me to take
my own life. I tell him all of this; surprisingly
he isn't judgmental. He asks me
what my goals are in our sessions together, a question
never considered. I say, I just want to be able to work out

all of the old memories I've blocked out, even
from myself, like a magician whose best tricks
are left in a trunk he cannot open. I want to

let all the attractions out so I can see
what needs to be fixed, what I've been
neglecting inside of myself while
I've been entertaining the time of others.

Proposal

She will be worth staying up
until three in the morning cramped in a car

two hours away from home so you can do
what you came there to do. She will be
worth the nervousness you feel

calling her father on the phone to ask
for his blessing, asking that he take her
back to his home so you can do

what you will travel all that way
to do. She will be worth it because
if you are going to propose to her

it doesn't matter how, you've already spent
so much time awake talking to her while
she's an ocean and four, maybe five time zones away. All

of the time, all of the terrible horror movies you will watch
together, all of the late nights where you're a black boy
with a pocket full of nothing but her cell phone number

texting you to let her know when you got home
because your life can become a horror movie
in the blink of an eye. All of the forgiveness, all of the tears.

Worth it. Even when she becomes insane
about the wedding, becomes crazy over the engagement, worth it
because she knows black people don't get to win often, don't

get to celebrate much. You two are a celebration, a victory
to be defended and it's worth it. In this world where men
with Batman's guilty pleasure want to claim everything,

want to call themselves heroes every time our lives are taken
and our names are turned into possessions

buried in the back of the the museums for white privilege,
worth it. People will want to take her because that's what they do

to black girls who are too bright to be buried like dead nations.
Her skin absorbs so much sunlight her kisses make you glow
and you have never known what it felt like to be the moon

before. She will be worth it, so you say her name
like you are pledging allegiance. Say her name like

you are the last person to speak its language. Say
her name like it is your wife's, and no man can conquer that.

Elephant in the Room

My depression is the elephant in the room,
everyone sees it but nobody moves
out of fear that it will stampede

over everything. This mammoth
towering above everyone I love
with its memory of the circus,
of all things me, terrorizes the tents

holding the performers. Even the clowns
of my past, my ex-girlfriends
have had to deal with it because
when black and in love this mastodon
stays present, stays one wrong turn, one phone call

to the police away. It will kill you
and think nothing of it as it moves on

to the next black body whose house
it can occupy. But I've found someone
worth fighting the ivory tusks of depression
for. She knows firsthand how difficult it can be

going on with this giant on your back, always
lugging around your past, using it against you
when you're down but we know that it will get
better. At times it will be hard to do but when
the elephant in the room emerges we will be

together to tame the beast,
to burn its bones and fossilize the ashes.

Tornadoes

In Tupelo, Mississippi,
my fiancée and I see
three confederate flags. Water

of course is wet. A few weeks
prior to this trip she embraces me,
crying, asking me not to leave
the house. I do not oblige her. Water

after all is still wet. A few weeks prior
to this trip another black man
lays there, dead, shot in the street
by the police. And another. And
another. I have grown numb to it

all at this point. We are passing
through Indiana on the way back
and there is a tornado touching down.
I feel safer, less on edge. Know the cop

cars aren't gonna come for us now. I wish
every day was a tornado watch. Water is still wet

in this equation and America is still
America. Which is to say that if America,
just as racist as it has ever been,
elects a bigot in the fall and I am not

surprised in the slightest. This week
while driving for Uber I picked up
three cops who bragged about dating
underaged women and yet another
black man was shot in the street. Water is wet

and I am flooded with emotion. Every week
I am reminded of how my presence isn't wanted
in my own home country and I have to swallow
that truth like a glass of water. I gulp it down

and nearly suffocate every time. I wish every week
there were tornadoes touching down, hurling
squad cars left and right just so we could feel safer
for once. I wish there were storms brewing for all

the racists present and we could just speed on
through it, just fast forward to the future
where this country isn't bigoted. But that tomorrow
never comes. Water is still wet. America is still
America. There will still be people who view

my life as threat before gunmen, or cops. The police
will still function for the sole purpose of hunting
us black people. In Tupelo, Mississippi, we celebrated
a wedding, despite it all. We found joy despite it all,

and in Memphis, Tennessee, me and my sister reunited. We
celebrated this reunion despite it all. We will celebrate
despite it all because they can't take our joy from us

while we still have it. Water may be wet but the music
stays fine enough to dance to and we gonna keep on dancing
until the rug is cut and our feet are falling off our ankles.

Acknowledgments

The author thanks, appreciates, and acknowledges the following publications in which poems from this collection previously appeared:

Damfino Press: "Pegasus"

Emerge Literary Journal: "Gossip Girl"

Eunoia Review: "Huntsville," "Silent Moments," and "The Door Was Left Unlocked for Someone Else"

Indiana Voice Journal: "Disappearing Search" and "Raven"

Juncture Review: "Grocery Bags"

Mobius: The Journal for Social Change: "Henry Ford Hospital, 2007," "Trumpet," and "London, May 2016"

One Sentence Poems: "Traffic" and "Cellular"

Pittsburgh Poetry Review: "The Firebreather Speaks of Spells," "Handshakes with Firearms," and "Offerings"

Stone Path Review: "The Firebreather Speaks of Stockholm Syndrome"

The Missing Slate: "Tornadoes"

Word Riot: "Negotiating Loss" and "Cloaking"

Special Thanks

I want to thank my family for inspiring many of these poems, and my ex-fiancée for the person she was while we were engaged.

Post Credit Scene, Letter to Jamaal May

Jamaal, this manuscript started
as a response to a publisher

looking at another manuscript
and telling me I was like you
only not as refined. Isn't that too
a kind of blackness, to be confused
for another because after all we do
all look alike? I'm certain that isn't

what they meant when they passed
on my manuscript, offering critical feedback
and honestly I had taken it as a compliment
to be compared to you. In the months since then

I faced my depression and proposed to my lover
and she said yes. I'm so thankful, and so blessed

for everything that has come into my life and will
come into my life. That too is a kind of blackness,
to be so spiritually inclined every single thing is a reason
for giving thanks. Even another day on this planet

convinced that it doesn't want us here, is blessing
enough. Jamaal, if you're reading this I want to thank you

for being the inspiration and mentor you have always been.
You are one of my many brothers and although I know
the mastodon is not buried, will not stay dead long, and my depression
will rear its head again, I know I've been raised by a strong village.

Contents

Big Top

Dinner Discussions	4
Trumpet	5
Employment Application	6
Newport News	7
Huntsville	8
The Firebreather Speaks of Spells	9
Pegasus	10
Henry Ford Hospital, 2007	11
Circus, 2002	12

The Juggler

The Juggler Speaks of Work	16
Stolen	17
Raven	18
Disappearing Search	19
Traffic	20
The Firebreather Speaks of Prayer	21
Cellular	22
Shadow Lounge, Oakland, 2015	23
Onions	24

The Tightrope Walker

The Tightrope Walker Speaks of Becoming a Trapeze Artist	28
Negotiating Loss	29
Disappointing My Mother	30
Sweetness	31
Wounds	32
Swallowing Grief	33
Gradual Transformations	34

The Clowns

The Clowns Speak of the Firebreather	38
Gossip Girl	39
The Door Was Left Unlocked for Someone Else	40
Forbidden	41
The Firebreather Speaks of Stockholm Syndrome	42
The Summoning	43
Offerings	44
Cloaking	45

The Animal Tamer

The Animal Tamer Speaks of Training	50
When Trying to Create a Distraction from the Food Falling Off My Fork	52
Firefly	54
Grocery Bags	55
The Firebreather Speaks of Rescue	56
Consumption	57
Silent Moments	58
Black Family	59
New Years in New Orleans	61
London, May 2016	62
Howl	65
How I Almost Got Killed	66
Demons	68
Handshakes with Firearms	69
Gravity	71
Melt	72
My Little Brother Comes Back from San Antonio	74
Circus, 2016	77
Proposal	78
Elephant in the Room	80
Tornadoes	81
Post Credit Scene, Letter to Jamaal May	85

www.ingramcontent.com/pod-product-compliance
Lightning Source LLC
Chambersburg PA
CBHW021447080526
44588CB00009B/735